COOKING *with the* UGLESICHES

COOKING *with the* UGLESICHES

BY JOHN UGLESICH

PELICAN PUBLISHING COMPANY
Gretna 2008

The word "Pelican" and the depiction of a pelican are trademarks
of Pelican Publishing Company, Inc., and are registered
in the U.S. Patent and Trademark Office.

Library of Congress Cataloging-in-Publication Data

Uglesich, John.
  Cooking with the Uglesiches / by John Uglesich.
      p. cm.
  Includes index.
    ISBN 978-1-58980-551-4 (hardcover : alk. paper) 1. Cookery (Seafood) 2.
Cookery, American—Louisiana style. 3. Cookery—Louisiana—New
Orleans. 4. Uglesich's Restaurant. I. Title.
  TX747.U3365 2008
  641.6′92—dc22

                                       2007047395

Food photography by Phil Luchsinger, unless otherwise noted

Printed in Singapore
Published by Pelican Publishing Company, Inc.
1000 Burmaster Street, Gretna, Louisiana 70053

To Princess Katherine Corleone Scarlet Uglesich (Katie).
I miss your big brown eyes, that bark, and your love.
You truly were one of a kind.
—John Uglesich

To Josephine N. Flettrich. There is not a day that goes by that
I don't think of you. I know you are with Daddy and Katie
in a better place looking down on us.
—Gail Uglesich

To Emily Uglesich. I love and miss you. All of your
fabulous recipes were in your head. I only wish you
could have shared them with me.
—Anthony Uglesich

Contents

An Open Letter

There are not enough words to express our sincere appreciation to the thousands of customers who have enjoyed our food. Managing and working every day in the restaurant business is hard work, but it has given us the opportunity to meet and become friends with so many people around the world.

To the people in the surrounding New Orleans area, your strength and determination are what make New Orleans one of the most unique cities in the world. We are New Orleans born and New Orleans proud. We always purchased and served fresh Louisiana seafood. Giving back to our community included signing contracts with local companies such as our publishing company and our supplier for our T-shirts, hats, aprons, and pot holders.

To all of our customers, we love and miss each of you.

Anthony and Gail Uglesich

John and his wife, Iuliana, at the New Orleans Jazz and Heritage Festival book tent, with the first cookbook.

John and his sister Donna, at the New Orleans Jazz and Heritage Festival book tent. All copies of Uglesich's Restaurant Cookbook *were sold.*

Acknowledgments

To my wife, Iuliana Patrascu Uglesich, you are the most beautiful woman in the world both inside and outside! I truly respect you and look forward to spending the rest of our lives together. You make me complete and the happiest person. *Te iubesc. Tu esti dragostra vietii mele.*

To my parents, Gail and Anthony, thank you again for believing in me to write the second book. Without your dedication and hard work, I would not have this opportunity. I have lived my dream by writing these books. I could not ask for two better and more loving parents.

To my sister Donna, thank you so much for being my friend and for always watching over me.

To all of my family and friends, your love and support have not gone unnoticed.

Thanks to all of the employees of Pelican Publishing Company. It has been an honor and privilege to work so closely with each of you.

Thanks to my personal editors, my sistas, Donna and Dynell.

Thanks to Phil and Judy Luchsinger. Your pictures are wonderful.

Thanks to Chalon, Nancy, Ray, and Ellen. Your pictures for the last day are awesome.

J.R., that's what I'm talking about.

Jay Jones, there are not enough words to thank you for all of your work on the Web page. One day, my friend, we will meet.

To all of my Romanian friends in Memphis: *La Multi Ani!*

Thanks to all the employees who have worked at the restaurant.

To Mama Mariana, Tata Florin, Daniel, Marius, Milie, Eva, and

Maya, thank you so much for making me feel so welcomed. I am proud to be part of your family.

Daniel, my brother, you are a good man.

Introduction

Cooking with the Uglesiches, the highly anticipated sequel to *Uglesich's Restaurant Cookbook,* focuses on recipes from the restaurant that were not included in the first book, as well as Anthony and Gail's own creations at home. While the restaurant offered Creole seafood dishes, Anthony and Gail like to prepare Italian and traditional American meals in their home.

The restaurant never offered desserts, yet this book provides some simple and popular desserts prepared by different family members.

Also in this book, take a pictorial tour of Uglesich's last full day in business, as seen through the eyes of the customers.

Finally, many people have seen the destruction that Hurricane Katrina brought to this region, yet *Cooking with the Uglesiches* provides a different glimpse of the storm's aftermath—the outreach, love, and support offered by the Uglesich's customers. Read the e-mails received during this trying time, when Anthony and Gail did not know the status of their house or restaurant property. They continued to receive daily e-mails from loyal customers offering them a house, money, or prayers.

This book will be treasured by anyone who has dined at the restaurant, as well as those who have heard about the restaurant but were never fortunate enough to have dined with Mr. Tony and Ms. Gail.

ABBREVIATIONS

Standard

tsp.	=	teaspoon
tbsp.	=	tablespoon
oz.	=	ounce
qt.	=	quart
lb.	=	pound

Metric

ml.	=	milliliter
l.	=	liter
g.	=	gram
kg.	=	kilogram
mg.	=	milligram

STANDARD-METRIC APPROXIMATIONS

$1/8$ teaspoon	=	.6 milliliter		
$1/4$ teaspoon	=	1.2 milliliters		
$1/2$ teaspoon	=	2.5 milliliters		
1 teaspoon	=	5 milliliters		
1 tablespoon	=	15 milliliters		
4 tablespoons	=	$1/4$ cup	=	60 milliliters
8 tablespoons	=	$1/2$ cup	=	118 milliliters
16 tablespoons	=	1 cup	=	236 milliliters
2 cups	=	473 milliliters		
2 $1/2$ cups	=	563 milliliters		
4 cups	=	946 milliliters		
1 quart	=	4 cups	=	.94 liter

SOLID MEASUREMENTS

$1/2$ ounce	=	15 grams		
1 ounce	=	25 grams		
4 ounces	=	110 grams		
16 ounces	=	1 pound	=	454 grams

COOKING *with the* UGLESICHES

Chapter One

Recipes from the Restaurant

Following are seafood creations from the restaurant, as well as new additions from Anthony and Gail.

Crab Fricassee

This recipe was a special served in the restaurant.

2 tbsp. vegetable oil
2 tbsp. flour
6 scallions, minced
4 cloves garlic, minced
1 red bell pepper, minced
2 stalks celery, minced
2 tbsp. tomato paste
5 cups water
1 lb. shrimp, peeled and deveined
1 lb. crabmeat
2 tsp. salt
$\frac{1}{2}$ tsp. black pepper
$\frac{1}{4}$ tsp. cayenne
$\frac{1}{4}$ tsp. dried thyme leaves
$\frac{1}{2}$ tsp. dried basil
3 tbsp. chopped parsley
2 tbsp. sherry
Cooked rice

First prepare a roux. To do this, heat a saucepan over medium/low heat, and pour in the oil. Slowly add the flour, and constantly stir, until golden brown.

Add the scallions, garlic, red pepper, and celery. Sauté for 5 minutes.

Add the tomato paste, and cook for 3 minutes.

Slowly add 3 cups water. Stir well, and let cool for 20 minutes.

Add the shrimp, crabmeat, salt, pepper, cayenne, thyme, basil, and 2 cups water.

Cook for 10 minutes.

Remove from the heat.

Stir in the parsley and sherry.

Pour over a bowl of rice.

Serves 12.

Crabmeat Louie

1 cup mayonnaise
$\frac{1}{2}$ cup sour cream
$\frac{1}{4}$ cup Heinz™ chili sauce
2 tbsp. lemon juice
$\frac{1}{4}$ cup diced green bell pepper
2 to 4 tbsp. chopped chives
1 tsp. salt
$\frac{1}{4}$ tsp. black pepper
$\frac{1}{8}$ tsp. cayenne
2 tbsp. chopped parsley
1 lb. crabmeat, lump or claw
Lettuce

Mix all of the above ingredients, except the crabmeat, in a bowl.

Place crabmeat on top of a bed of lettuce.

Place the desire amount of dressing on top.

Ecstasy

*Gail likes to
use Danish
blue cheese.*

*The extra
sauce can be
refrigerated.*

This appetizer of shrimp sautéed in a sauce and served over a bed of lettuce with a blue cheese dip on the side was very poplar at Uglesich's.

1 cup crumbled blue cheese
²/₃ cup extra-virgin olive oil
2 tsp. fresh lemon juice
³/₄ cup heavy cream
3 tbsp. minced garlic
¹/₂ cup chopped parsley
¹/₄ cup medium-dry sherry
2 to 4 tbsp. hot sauce
2 tbsp. fresh lime juice
8 medium shrimp with tails, peeled and deveined
Lettuce

Puree the blue cheese, ¹/₃ cup oil, lemon juice, and cream in a food processor until smooth.

Transfer to a serving cup.

Place the garlic, parsley, ¹/₃ cup oil, sherry, hot sauce, and lime juice in a bowl and stir.

Pour some of the sauce into a skillet and set on medium heat.

Place the shrimp in the skillet. Sauté until the shrimp turn pink on both sides.

Place the shrimp on top of the lettuce on a plate. Place the cup of blue cheese dip on the side.

Serves 2.

Purgatory

Anthony gave this name to this shrimp appetizer because the butter sauce is hot. The recipe is a three-step process.

Sauce

1 stick unsalted butter or margarine
1 tsp. salt
1 tsp. cayenne
4 tsp. hot sauce

Melt the butter.

Add the salt, cayenne, and hot sauce and stir.

Shrimp

Vegetable oil
1 lb. large shrimp with tails, peeled and deveined
Breadcrumbs

Pour oil in a fryer and set on medium heat.

Dip the shrimp in breadcrumbs.

Fry the shrimp in hot oil until golden brown.

Toss the fried shrimp in the above sauce.

Gorgonzola Sauce

4 oz. gorgonzola cheese
1 cup mayonnaise
1 container (8 oz.) sour cream
1 to 2 tbsp. fat-free milk
$1\frac{1}{2}$ tsp. salt
$\frac{1}{4}$ tsp. black pepper
$\frac{1}{4}$ tsp. Worcestershire sauce

Note

The extra sauces can be refrigerated and reused.

Puree all the ingredients in a food processor.

Place the shrimp on a plate, and drizzle some of the gorgonzola sauce on top.

Serves 8.

Uggilous

This Asian-influenced shrimp dish is a good appetizer with some sweetness and heat. One customer liked to have the sauce over pasta.

1 tbsp. light brown sugar
4 tsp. rice wine vinegar
1 (12 oz.) jar apricot preserves
1 cup plum sauce
1 tbsp. minced shallot
1 tsp. minced garlic
$\frac{1}{2}$ tsp. minced ginger
$\frac{1}{4}$ tsp. crushed red pepper flakes
1 tbsp. sambal chili paste
Pinch salt
6 medium shrimp with tails, peeled and deveined

In a large bowl, dissolve the sugar into the rice wine vinegar, and slowly add the rest of the ingredients, except the shrimp.

Place some sauce in a skillet and set on medium heat.

Place the shrimp in the skillet and sauté until they turn pink.

Serves 2.

Sambal can be found in Asian food stores.

Large shrimp can be used instead of medium shrimp.

The sauce stores well in the refrigerator.

Whatcha Doin' Shrimp

This recipe is named after one of Anthony and Gail's nieces, who always answers the phone with: "Whatcha doin'?" Both she and her husband were nice enough to take us into their home upon our evacuation from Hurricane Katrina.

Salt
Black pepper
$\frac{1}{2}$ lb. medium shrimp with tails, peeled and deveined
2 tbsp. extra-virgin olive oil
6 cloves garlic, thinly sliced
$\frac{1}{2}$ tbsp. rice wine vinegar
Pinch crushed red pepper flakes
$\frac{1}{2}$ tbsp. lemon zest
1 tbsp. lemon juice
1 tbsp. chopped parsley

Salt and pepper the shrimp.

Pour the oil in an 8-in. skillet, and set on medium heat.

Place the garlic in the skillet and cook until it turns golden, but do not burn.

Place the shrimp in the skillet and cook for approximately 2 minutes on each side, or until pink.

While the shrimp are cooking, add the vinegar, red pepper flakes, lemon zest, lemon juice, and parsley.

Serves 4.

Keeping the tails on the shrimp helps to prevent shrinkage.

Stuffed Eggs with Shrimp

6 eggs
$\frac{1}{2}$ lb. small shrimp, peeled and deveined
$\frac{1}{2}$ tsp. salt
$\frac{1}{8}$ tsp. black pepper
Pinch cayenne
1 tbsp. minced celery
1 tbsp. minced onion
2 to 4 tbsp. mayonnaise
1 tbsp. yellow mustard
1 dill pickle, minced
Chopped parsley

Hard-boil the eggs. When cool, peel the eggs and cut the eggs in half lengthwise.

Take out the yolks and place them in a bowl. Set aside the egg whites.

Mash the yolks.

Spray a skillet with nonstick cooking spray.

Season the shrimp with salt, pepper, and cayenne.

Sauté the shrimp over medium heat until they turn pink.

Dice the shrimp and place in the bowl with the mashed yolks.

Add the celery, onion, mayonnaise, mustard, and pickle. Mix well. Add salt and pepper to taste.

Mound some of the shrimp stuffing inside the hollow of each egg white.

Sprinkle some parsley on top of each stuffed egg.

Serves 6.

Oysters Pesto

These oysters make a good appetizer and are wonderful to serve at a party.

1 bottle (2.5 oz.) pine nuts
1 cup basil leaves
$1/2$ cup fresh spinach leaves
6 stems curly parsley
3 stems marjoram
6 cloves garlic
$1/3$ cup grated imported Parmesan cheese
$1/3$ cup grated imported Romano cheese
$1/4$ tsp. salt
$1/4$ tsp. black pepper
$1/2$ cup extra-virgin olive oil
Oysters

Roast the pine nuts by placing them on a baking pan in the oven at 350 degrees for 5 to 10 minutes.

Place the basil, spinach, parsley, marjoram, garlic, cheeses, salt, pepper, and roasted pine nuts into a food processor.

Grind on low speed, and slowly pour in the oil.

Place each oyster on an oyster shell, and top with the sauce. Then place on a baking pan.

Bake at 350 degrees for approximately 5 minutes or until the edges of the oysters curl. The oysters can also be broiled in the oven.

Serves 20.

Oyster Supreme

This appetizer features oysters that are dipped in buttermilk and flour, fried, and then served with a Gruyere sauce.

3 cups heavy cream
4 tsp. cornstarch
4 tbsp. unsalted margarine or butter, cut into pieces
2 cups shredded Gruyere cheese
1 tsp. salt
1 tsp. black pepper
1 tsp. cayenne
4 tsp. Pernod™
Oysters
Buttermilk
Flour
Vegetable oil

Set a saucepan on medium heat.

Add the cream and cornstarch.

Constantly stir. Add the margarine, piece by piece.

Let the sauce come to a slow boil. Remove from the fire and add the cheese.

When the cheese melts, season the sauce with salt, pepper, cayenne, and Pernod™.

Dip the oysters in buttermilk, and then dredge in flour. Deep-fry the oysters in hot oil until they float and dance on the top and are golden brown.

Drain the oysters. Pour the sauce on top.

Serves 12.

Hakon

The dish was named for a longtime friend, who when he could not remember a word used this made-up word instead. The item was a side dish served in the restaurant many years ago.

1 stick butter
1 large onion, chopped
1 large green bell pepper, chopped
4 Roma tomatoes, cored, seeded, and chopped
4 cans (15$\frac{1}{2}$ oz.) creamed corn
Salt
Black pepper

Set a saucepan on medium heat, and melt the butter in it.

Add the onion and bell pepper. Sauté for 5 minutes.

Add the tomatoes and corn. Cook on low heat for about 15 minutes.

Add salt and pepper to taste.

Serves 10.

Succotash

This makes a great side dish for your main course.

Vegetable oil
1 green bell pepper, chopped
1 large Vidalia onion, chopped
2 large Creole tomatoes, chopped
1 lb. fresh okra, thinly sliced
1 clove garlic, chopped
4 ears white corn
1 lb. shrimp, peeled and deveined
Salt
Black pepper
Chopped parsley

Notes

If Creole tomatoes are not available, a different type of tomato can be used.

Hot sauce or cayenne can be added for more seasoning.

Succotash

Pour the oil into a skillet, and set on medium heat.

Add the bell pepper, onion, tomatoes, okra, and garlic.

Cook until the okra is no longer stringy, 45 minutes to 1 hour.

Take the kernels off the corn and add to the skillet. Cook for approximately 15 minutes.

Add the shrimp and cook for 2 to 3 minutes or until they turn pink.

Season with salt and pepper.

Sprinkle parsley on top.

Serves 8.

Angry Shrimp

This dish is served on top of white rice. Prepare the sauce first, then cook the shrimp in the sauce.

2 sticks margarine or butter
3 tbsp. canola oil
15 cloves garlic, thinly sliced
1 red bell pepper, sliced
1 yellow bell pepper, sliced
1 green bell pepper, sliced
$1/4$ cup Chinese chili sauce
8 shrimp with tails, peeled and deveined

Set a skillet on medium heat, and melt the margarine.

Add the oil.

Place the garlic, bell peppers, and chili sauce into the skillet.

Stir everything.

Set another skillet on medium heat, and pour the desired amount of sauce into the bottom of it.

Place the shrimp in the pan and cook until they turn pink.

Serve over white rice.

Serves 1.

Notes

The sauce can be made a couple of days in advance and refrigerated.

The longer the sauce sits, the better it tastes.

The extra sauce can be refrigerated and will last as long as the expiration date of the margarine or butter.

Shrimp Etouffée

Gail found a good recipe for shrimp étouffée in Leon Soniat's cookbook, *La Bouche Creole*. She adapted the seasonings when she served this dish in the restaurant. It is served over rice.

6 tbsp. vegetable oil
6 tbsp. flour
1 large onion, chopped
1 green bell pepper, chopped
4 stalks celery, chopped
4 cloves garlic, chopped
1 can (6 oz.) tomato paste
2 cans (10½ oz.) beef consommé
2+ cups water
3 bay leaves
1 tsp. dried basil
½ tsp. dried thyme leaves
1 tsp. chili powder
¼ + ⅛ tsp. cayenne
¾ tsp. black pepper
1 tbsp. salt
3 lb. shrimp, peeled and deveined
1 bunch scallions, chopped
2 tbsp. chopped parsley

Pour the oil in a pot, and set on medium-low heat.

Slowly add the flour, and constantly stir, until the roux turns brown.

Reduce the heat to low and simmer the roux. Add the onion, bell pepper, celery, and garlic. Sauté for 10 to 15 minutes.

Add the tomato paste and mix well.

Add the beef consommé and 2 cups water. Cook for 5 minutes.

Add the bay leaves, basil, thyme, chili powder, cayenne, black pepper, and salt. Continue to simmer on low heat for 45 minutes to 1 hour.

Add the shrimp, scallions, and parsley and simmer for 20 minutes.

Remove from the heat and let the seasonings blend.

Taste to adjust seasonings or water.

Serves 12.

Shrimp Etouffée

Shrimp Giada

This recipe was inspired by Giada De Laurentiis, the popular cook-book author and television chef.

1 lb. large shrimp with tails, peeled and deveined
1 tsp. salt
$^1/_4$ tsp. black pepper
$^1/_8$ tsp. crushed red pepper flakes
3 to 4 tbsp. olive oil
1 medium onion, chopped
4 cloves garlic, chopped
1 can (14$^1/_2$ oz.) diced tomatoes
1 cup dry white wine
1 tsp. chopped oregano
3 to 4 tbsp. chopped basil
3 to 4 tbsp. chopped parsley

In the morning, place the shrimp in a bowl, and season with salt, pepper, and red pepper flakes.

Cover the bowl with plastic wrap and marinate in the refrigerator.

When you are ready to cook, pour the oil into a skillet and set on medium heat.

Sauté the shrimp in the skillet until they turn pink.

Remove the shrimp.

In the same skillet, sauté the onion and garlic, about 5 minutes, but do not burn.

Add the tomatoes, wine, oregano, and basil.

Stir together and cook for about 10 minutes.

Place the shrimp back into the skillet, stir to mix, and sprinkle the parsley on top.

Cook for 1 to 2 minutes to reheat the shrimp.

Serves 4 to 5.

Shrimp Giada

That's What I'm Talking About

This recipe is named after a relative's favorite saying. It is a spicy dish that requires no salt, as there is enough sodium in the ingredients.

Sauce

1 cup mayonnaise
¼ cup apricot preserves
1 tbsp. soy sauce
1 tbsp. Dijon mustard
1 clove garlic, minced
½ tsp. grated ginger
1 tsp. chili paste

In the morning, stir all the ingredients together and refrigerate.

Shrimp

1½ lb. shrimp with tails, peeled and deveined
⅛ tsp. black pepper
Pinch cayenne

When you are ready to cook, place the shrimp in a bowl, and season with the pepper and cayenne.

Take 1 to 2 tbsp. sauce and mix with the shrimp in the bowl.

Spray a skillet with nonstick cooking spray. When it is hot, pour all the contents of the bowl into the skillet. Cook the shrimp for approximately 2 minutes on each side, or until the shrimp turn pink. Remove the shrimp from the skillet, and place on a plate. Serve the remaining sauce in a small dipping bowl alongside the shrimp.

Serves 4.

Notes

The chili paste can be purchased at any Asian food store. We use sambal.

Keeping the tails on the shrimp helps to prevent shrinkage.

Seafood Gumbo

1/4 cup vegetable oil
1/2 cup flour
2 tbsp. canola oil
2 lb. frozen okra
1 large onion, chopped
2 stalks celery, chopped
1 medium green bell pepper, chopped
6 scallions, chopped
2 cloves garlic, chopped
1 can (6 oz.) tomato paste
1 can (28 oz.) crushed tomatoes
1 tbsp. salt
1/2 tsp. black pepper
1 tsp. fresh thyme leaves
1/4 tsp. cayenne
2 to 3 bay leaves
1 tsp. hot sauce
1 tbsp. Worcestershire sauce
8 cups water
2 lb. small raw shrimp
1 lb. lump crabmeat
2 tbsp. chopped parsley
Cooked white rice
Chopped parsely for garnish

Notes

Canola oil can be used for the roux.

It takes a long time to make a roux correctly. Stir frequently, so as not to burn the flour.

Leftover gumbo can be refrigerated, or it can be frozen if not used within a week.

Pour the oil in a stockpot that has a lid, and set it on medium heat.

When the oil is hot, add the flour, and stir.

Reduce the heat to low and cook for 45 minutes to 1 hour to make a dark brown roux.

While the roux is cooking, pour the canola oil into a skillet, and cook the okra for about 30 minutes or until it is no longer stringy.

Add the onions, celery, bell pepper, scallions, and garlic to the roux.

Sauté for approximately 5 minutes.

Then add the tomato paste and crushed tomatoes. Cook for approximately 10 minutes.

Add the salt, pepper, thyme, cayenne, bay leaves, hot sauce,

Worcestershire sauce, and cooked okra. Mix all together.

Slowly add the water.

Bring the mixture to a boil.

Add the shrimp, lower the heat, and cook covered for 30 minutes.

Uncover the pot. Add the crabmeat and parsley. Cover the pot and cook for approximately 15 minutes.

Place a little white rice in each bowl, pour some of the gumbo on top, and garnish with parsley.

Serves 12.

Artichoke and Oyster Soup

Notes

Use small oysters.

Mascarpone cheese is in the mozzarella cheese family.

If the soup is too thick, add more chicken broth.

2 tbsp. extra-virgin olive oil
1 bunch scallions, chopped
2 cloves garlic, chopped
1 pkg. (9 oz.) frozen artichoke hearts, thawed
4 cups low-sodium chicken broth
1 pt. oysters
$^1/_2$ cup mascarpone cheese
2 tbsp. chopped parsley
Salt
Black pepper

Heat the oil in a stockpot over medium heat.

Add the scallions and garlic. Sauté for about 2 minutes.

Add the artichoke hearts and sauté for 2 to 3 minutes.

Add the chicken broth.

When the broth is hot, add the oysters with liquid, and cook until the edges curl.

Add the mascarpone cheese.

Add the parsley. Add salt and pepper to taste.

Stir and cook until the cheese melts.

Serves 4 to 6.

Crawfish Creole

Gail was inspired to make this dish by a recipe in the local newspaper, the *Times-Picayune*. She made it her own by creating her own seasonings.

$^1/_2$ cup vegetable oil
1 cup flour
1 onion, chopped
4 stalks celery, chopped
1 small red bell pepper, chopped
3 cloves garlic, chopped
1 can (28 oz.) crushed tomatoes
1 can (6 oz.) tomato paste
4 to 6 cups water
1 tsp. Worcestershire sauce
1 tbsp. salt
$^3/_4$ tsp. black pepper
$^1/_4$ tsp. cayenne
3 lb. crawfish tails, peeled
2 tbsp. chopped scallions
2 tbsp. chopped parsley
Cooked rice

First make a roux. Set a pot on medium-low heat, and pour in the oil. Slowly add the flour and constantly stir until golden brown.

Add the onion, celery, bell pepper, and garlic. Sauté for 5 to 10 minutes.

Add the tomatoes and paste, mix well, and cook for 5 minutes.

Add 4 cups water, and bring to a boil. Lower the heat, and simmer for 1 hour.

Add the Worcestershire, salt, pepper, and cayenne. Stir well.

Note

If you wish to make the sauce thinner, then add more cups of water.

Add the crawfish tails, and cook for 15 minutes.

Add the scallions and parsley. Stir well.

Serve over a bowl of rice.

Serves 8.

Catfish Piccata

This recipe was born when Anthony and Gail were watching TV and saw Giada De Laurentiis prepare chicken piccata on her cooking show. They decided to substitute catfish for the chicken.

1 tsp. salt
$1/4$ tsp. black pepper
Catfish fillets (1 lb. total)
All-purpose flour
4 tbsp. butter or margarine
2 tbsp. extra-virgin olive oil
$1/2$ cup low-sodium chicken broth
$1/4$ cup fresh lemon juice
$1/4$ cup capers, rinsed
2 tbsp. chopped parsley

Salt and pepper the catfish, then dredge in flour.

Set a skillet on medium heat, and melt the butter.

Add the oil.

Place the catfish in the skillet. Cook the catfish on each side for approximately 2 minutes or until the fillets are golden brown.

Remove the catfish from the skillet. Drain on paper towels.

Add the chicken broth, lemon juice, capers, and parsley to the skillet. Bring to a boil.

Cook for 1 minute. Scrape the bottom of the skillet to loosen any brown bits.

Turn off the heat, and add the catfish back to the skillet.

Stir for 2 minutes to heat in the sauce.

Serves 4.

Catfish Piccata

Chapter Two

Recipes from Home

Following are recipes that Anthony and Gail prepare in their own home.

47

Bayou Swamp

1 stick + 4 tbsp. butter
4 tbsp. flour
1 cup half-and-half
1 cup heavy cream
$1/2$ cup ketchup
4 oz. fresh white mushrooms, sliced
2 lb. crawfish tails
1 bunch scallions, chopped
$1/4$ cup brandy
2 tsp. salt
$1/2$ tsp. black pepper
$1/4$ tsp. cayenne

On medium-low heat, melt 4 tbsp. butter in a pot and add the flour. Cook until golden brown.

Slowly add the half-and-half and cream. Stir constantly until the sauce thickens.

Add the ketchup, mushrooms, and crawfish tails. Cook for 2 minutes.

In another skillet, melt the remaining butter and sauté the scallions.

Add the scallions to the crawfish mixture.

Add the brandy, salt, pepper, and cayenne. Cook for 5 minutes.

Place the mixture in a casserole dish, and bake for 15 minutes at 325 degrees.

Serves 8.

Crawfish Dip

This is a great party dip. Anthony and Gail often make it for Super Bowl gatherings.

4 tbsp. butter
1 red bell pepper, chopped
1 small onion, chopped
$^{1}/_{4}$ cup chopped scallions
$^{1}/_{2}$ lb. Velveeta™ Mexican cheese, diced
1 can low-sodium cream of mushroom soup
1 lb. peeled crawfish tails
1$^{1}/_{2}$ cups cooked brown rice
1 small can fiesta corn
Salt
Black pepper
Cayenne

Melt the butter in a skillet over medium heat.

Add the bell pepper, onion, and scallions and cook for 5 minutes.

Add the cheese, soup, and crawfish tails.

Continue to cook until the cheese melts in the skillet.

Add the rice, corn, salt, pepper, and cayenne.

Stir and then pour into a dipping bowl surrounded by your favorite chips.

Serves 20.

Shrimp and Crab Bisque

Gail was inspired to create this recipe after reading a bisque article in *Saveur* magazine.

1 lb. raw shrimp
3 cups water
¼ cup brandy
½ cup dry white wine
1 small onion, chopped
2 stalks celery, chopped
1 medium carrot, peeled and diced
1 cup heavy cream
1 cup half-and-half
1 tbsp. butter
2 tsp. salt
½ tsp. black pepper
¼ tsp. cayenne
Dash Tabasco™
1 lb. lump crabmeat

Peel and devein the shrimp, while keeping the tails on. Place the shells in a stockpot.

Add the water, brandy, and wine.

Bring to a boil.

Reduce the heat, and simmer for 15 minutes.

Take out and discard the shells. Strain the broth back into the pot.

Add the onion, celery, and carrot and cook on medium heat for 30 minutes.

Add the shrimp, and cook until they turn pink.

Place the mixture in a food processor and puree.

Place the puree back into the pot and set on low heat.

Slowly add the cream and half-and-half.

Add the butter and let it melt.

Add the salt, pepper, cayenne, and Tabasco™.

Fold in the crabmeat and simmer for 3 to 4 minutes.

Taste to add more seasonings if needed.

Serves 8.

Sweet Pea and Shrimp Soup

¹/₂ stick butter or margarine
1 large onion, chopped
¹/₂ lb. ham, diced
1 large can (32 oz.) chicken broth
2 bags (10 oz.) frozen sweet peas
1 tsp. salt
¹/₄ tsp. white pepper
¹/₂ lb. cooked shrimp, diced

Melt the butter in a stockpot.

Add the onion and ham, and sauté for approximately 5 minutes.

Note

If the soup is too thick, add more chicken broth before serving it.

Sweet Pea and Shrimp Soup

Pour in the chicken broth and stir.

Add the peas, and cook on medium heat for 15 minutes.

Add the salt and pepper.

Let the mixture cool.

Place the mixture in a blender and puree.

Pour it back into the pot, and add the shrimp.

Stir and let the mixture simmer on low heat for 5 minutes.

Serves 8 to 10.

Stuffed Artichokes

4 artichokes
$^1/_2$ cup plain breadcrumbs
$^1/_2$ cup grated imported Romano cheese
12 cloves garlic, chopped
2 tbsp. chopped parsley
Salt
Black pepper
Extra-virgin olive oil
$^1/_2$ to 2 cups water

Note

Never submerge the stuffed artichokes in water.

A day before cooking, cut the stems off the artichokes.

Cut off about $^1/_4$ of the artichokes at the tops. Be sure to scrape the hairy choke out of each artichoke.

Wash each artichoke and let it drain upside down on a paper towel overnight.

The next day, prepare the stuffing. Place the breadcrumbs, cheese, garlic, parsley, salt, and pepper in a large bowl and mix with your hands.

Place the mixture between the leaves of each artichoke.

Place the artichokes in a Dutch oven and drizzle the leaves with oil.

Add the water to the bottom of the pot.

Place the pot on the stove on medium heat. When the water comes to a boil, place the cover on the pot, and reduce the heat to medium low.

The artichokes are done when you can easily pull off one of the leaves. Start testing 2 hours into cooking.

More water may need to be added.

Serves 4.

Spinach and Artichoke Dip

Note

*Any leftovers must
be refrigerated.*

There are many different versions of this dip. John saw a recipe for it in a magazine and tweaked the ingredients to his taste. He has prepared his version for his wife to bring to potluck lunches at work.

1 cup sour cream
1 cup mayonnaise
2 cups grated Parmesan cheese
1 can artichoke hearts, drained and chopped
1 pkg. (10 oz.) frozen spinach, thawed and squeezed dry

Mix all the ingredients in a bowl.

Pour the mixture into a baking dish.

Bake at 350 degrees for approximately 25 minutes or until the cheese is bubbly.

Serve with your favorite bread or crackers.

Serves 20.

Shrimp and Eggplant Dressing

4 to 6 medium eggplants
1 lb. shrimp, peeled and deveined
1 lb. lean ground pork
1 lb. lean ground beef
1 onion, chopped
2 stalks celery, chopped
$1/2$ medium bell pepper, chopped
$1/4$ to $1/2$ cup water or chicken broth
3 cups cooked white rice
2 tbsp. chopped parsley
$1/2$ tsp. chopped fresh thyme leaves
1 tbsp. salt
$1/2$ tsp. black pepper
$1/4$ tsp. cayenne

Peel and chop the eggplants, sprinkle with some salt, and let sit in a colander for 1 hour. Then rinse with cold water and pat dry with a paper towel.

Spray a deep skillet with nonstick cooking spray, and sauté the shrimp.

In a separate skillet that has a lid, sauté the pork and beef on medium heat until no longer pink.

Then place the onion, celery, and bell pepper in the skillet with the meat and sauté for about 5 minutes.

Add the eggplant and water or chicken broth. Cover the skillet.

Notes

The pork will release grease, so no oil is needed.

Add more chicken broth or water if the mixture is too dry.

Cook for 30 to 45 minutes on medium heat.

Add the rice.

Add the shrimp, parsley, and thyme.

Season with salt, pepper, and cayenne.

Stir and serve.

Serves 12.

Shrimp with Corn

1 tbsp. butter
1 tbsp. olive oil
1 lb. small shrimp, peeled and deveined
1 clove garlic, chopped
1 small onion, chopped
1 red bell pepper, chopped
1 cup corn kernels
$1/4$ cup medium sherry
$1/2$ cup heavy cream
1 tsp. salt
$1/4$ tsp. black pepper
$1/8$ tsp. cayenne
2 tsp. chopped parsley

In a pot, heat the butter and olive oil on a low fire.

Sauté the shrimp and remove from the pot when pink.

In the same pot, add the garlic, onion, bell pepper, and corn.

Cook on a low fire for 15 minutes.

Add the sherry. Bring the fire up and boil the sherry until it is reduced by half.

Lower the fire, and add the cream and shrimp.

Cook for 2 minutes.

Add the salt, pepper, and cayenne.

Place in a serving bowl and sprinkle the parsley on top.

Serves 8.

Note

You may use more cream. You can also substitute half-and-half.

Oysters Rockefeller Casserole

Gail prepares this dish as part of our dinner on New Year's Day.

Notes

A mashed anchovy can be substituted for the anchovy paste.

Any leftovers can be frozen in small portions.

10 dozen oysters
2 sticks butter or margarine
1 large onion, chopped
1 bunch scallions, chopped
4 stalks celery, chopped
2 cloves garlic, chopped
$1/4$ cup chopped parsley
$1/2$ to 1 tsp. thyme
Dash Worcestershire sauce
1 tsp. anchovy paste
$1/2$ to $3/4$ cup seasoned breadcrumbs
$1/4$ to $1/2$ cup grated Parmesan cheese
1 to 2 tbsp. Pernod™
6 pkg. (10 oz.) chopped spinach, cooked and squeezed dry
2 tsp. salt
$1/2$ tsp. black pepper
$1/4$ to $1/2$ tsp. cayenne

Drain the oysters and save the liquid.

Melt the butter in a large skillet set on medium heat.

Sauté the onion, scallions, celery, garlic, parsley, and thyme for approximately 5 minutes.

Add the Worcestershire sauce, anchovy paste, and breadcrumbs.

Cook for 5 minutes.

Add the oysters, oyster liquid, cheese, and Pernod™.

Cook until the oysters curl, then add the spinach.

Season with salt, pepper, and cayenne.

Place everything into a casserole or baking pan and place in a 375-degree oven.

Bake for 20 minutes or until bubbly.

Serves 12 to 14.

Potato Casserole

Gail makes this dish every New Year's Day.

Note

Gail does not use salt.

3 large Yukon gold potatoes, washed and halved
Softened butter
1 large onion, sliced
1 cup milk
1 can cream of mushroom soup
$^1/_2$ lb. mild cheddar or Velveeta™ cheese, sliced
$^1/_4$ cup grated Parmesan cheese
Pinch paprika
Salt (optional)

Set the potatoes into a pot of water and boil.

Do not overcook; after about 20 minutes, keep testing for doneness by sticking a fork in the potatoes.

Drain, cool, and peel the potatoes. Slice the potatoes (either thin or thick). Grease a casserole dish with butter.

Layer the bottom of the casserole with half of the potatoes and then half of the onions.

Mix the milk and soup in a bowl.

Pour half of the mixture on top of the potatoes and onions.

Top with half of the cheddar cheese.

Repeat these steps.

Sprinkle Parmesan cheese, paprika, and salt on top.

Bake at 350 degrees for 45 minutes or until the cheese is melted.

Serves 6.

Potato-Broccoli Casserole

2 large Yukon gold potatoes, washed and halved
1 lb. broccoli, cut up
$1/2$ to 1 cup low-sodium chicken broth
4 to 8 oz. Philadelphia Cream Cheese™, diced
1 stick butter
Salt
Black pepper
$1/4$ to $1/2$ cup shredded Parmesan cheese

Boil the potatoes until tender. Drain the potatoes, cool, peel, and mash in a bowl.

Meanwhile, steam the broccoli.

Place the broccoli in a food processor.

To the broccoli, add $1/2$ cup chicken broth, 4 oz. cream cheese, $1/2$ stick butter (in pieces), salt, and pepper. Puree. Add more broth and/or cream cheese if you desire.

Pour the puree over the mashed potatoes and mix.

Pour the mixture into a casserole dish. Bake at 350 degrees for 15 minutes.

Remove the casserole from the oven, add the remaining butter (in pieces), and stir.

Place the casserole back into the oven, and bake for another 15 minutes. Remove from the oven, and sprinkle the Parmesan cheese on top.

Place the casserole back into the oven. Bake for another 5 minutes, until the cheese turns golden brown.

Serves 6.

Notes

Any type of steamed vegetable can replace the broccoli in this recipe. For example, Gail has used peas.

Stuffed Baked Potatoes

6 large Yukon gold potatoes
$\frac{1}{2}$ to 1 stick butter
$\frac{1}{4}$ to $\frac{1}{2}$ cup milk
Salt
Black pepper
American or cheddar cheese, diced
Chopped parsley

Wash the potatoes. Pierce 2 or 3 times with a fork. Bake at 450 degrees for 45 minutes to 1 hour, or until fork tender.

Remove from the oven, and when they are cool, slice a piece lengthwise off each potato. Scoop the contents out of each potato, leaving the potato shells intact, and place the contents in a bowl.

Add the butter, milk, salt, and pepper to the bowl. Mix well to mash the potatoes.

Stuff this mixture back into the potato shells.

Place pieces of cheese into the tops of the potatoes.

Reduce the oven temperature to 350 degrees, place the stuffed potatoes on a baking pan, and bake them until the cheese melts.

Garnish with parsley.

Serves 6.

Broccoli Italian Style

1 bunch broccoli
2 tbsp. butter
2 tbsp. extra-virgin olive oil
3 cloves garlic, thinly sliced
Fresh grated Parmigiano-Reggiano cheese
Salt
Black pepper

Cut off the stalks of the broccoli, keeping only the florets.

Wash the broccoli and steam in a steamer.

Melt the butter in a skillet set on medium-low heat.

Add the olive oil and garlic and sauté until golden but not brown.

Notes

Pamigiano-Reggiano cheese can be found in your local grocery store. It is imported from Italy.

Gail does not use salt because the cheese has enough salt.

Broccoli Italian Style

Place the steamed broccoli in a bowl.

Pour the sauce over the steamed broccoli.

Sprinkle cheese on top.

Salt and pepper to taste.

Serves 6.

Cauliflower with Parmesan

Gail makes this recipe every Thanksgiving.

1 head cauliflower
Butter
Fresh grated Parmigiano-Reggiano cheese

Cauliflower with Parmesan

Cut the cauliflower into desired pieces.

Steam the cauliflower.

Grease a casserole dish with butter.

Place the steamed cauliflower into the casserole dish and dot with pieces of butter.

Sprinkle the cheese over the cauliflower.

Bake at 400 degrees for 20 minutes, or until brown on top.

Serves 8.

French Green Beans

1 lb. fresh green beans
2 tbsp. salt
1 tbsp. canola oil
1 small onion, diced
2 cloves garlic, chopped
$^1/_4$ lb. ham, diced
Black pepper
Cayenne

Snap off and discard the ends of the beans.

Place the beans and salt in a pot of water, and bring to a boil.

Cook until the beans turn tender.

Drain the beans.

Place the oil in the same pot. Add the onion, garlic, and ham and sauté on medium heat.

Place the beans back into the pot, add $^1/_4$ cup water, reduce the heat to low, and mix well.

Cook for 30 minutes.

Season to taste with pepper and cayenne.

Serves 4.

Mother's Favorite Spinach

4 pkg. (10 oz.) frozen chopped spinach
1 tbsp. butter
1 small onion, chopped
Pinch sugar
Salt
$^3/_4$ cup cream
1 egg
1 tbsp. flour

Cook the spinach according to package directions. Squeeze out any excess moisture.

In the same pot, set on low heat, and melt the butter.

Sauté the onion until limp.

Add the spinach, sugar, salt, and $^1/_2$ cup cream and cook for 5 minutes.

Put this mixture into a greased casserole dish.

In a separate bowl, beat the egg. Add the remaining cream and the flour, and mix well.

Pour this mixture on top of the spinach mixture and bake in a preheated 350-degree oven for 20 minutes.

Serves 8.

Cole Slaw

1 1/4 tsp. red-wine vinegar
1 1/2 tbsp. chopped parsley
1/4 cup sweet pickle relish
1/2 cup mayonnaise
1 1/4 tsp. yellow mustard
1/2 tsp. salt
1/4 tsp. black pepper
1/8 tsp. cayenne
1 1/2 tsp. sugar
Dash hot sauce
1/2 lb. cooked shrimp, diced
1/4 cup diced red onion
1/2 bag classic cole-slaw vegetable mix

Make the dressing first. In a small bowl, mix the vinegar, parsley, relish, mayonnaise, mustard, salt, pepper, cayenne, sugar, and hot sauce.

In a large bowl, mix the shrimp, onion, and cole-slaw mix.

Place the desired amount of dressing on the cole slaw and mix.

Serves 4 to 6.

Note

The extra dressing can be refrigerated.

Croutons

Gail likes to make croutons to mix with her salads.

Ciabatta bread
Olive oil

Preheat the oven to 400 degrees.

Cut the ciabatta bread into thick squares.

Drizzle olive oil over the bread.

Place on a baking sheet in the oven, and after 5 minutes check to see if toasty.

If not toasty, bake for another 5 minutes.

Glaze for Poultry

Gail uses this glaze every year over Thanksgiving turkey. It can also be used over chicken or Cornish hens.

1 can (16 oz.) cranberry sauce
2 jars (15$^1/_4$ oz.) free-stone sliced peaches

Place the ingredients in a blender, and puree.

Pour some of the glaze over the cooked poultry, and serve the rest in a small bowl for dipping.

Baby Back Ribs

Notes

Gail and Anthony like to use Master Choice™ in barbecue sauce.

Any leftovers can be kept in the refrigerator.

This recipe is one of Anthony's favorites. Gail saw something similar on a Reynolds Oven Bags™ box but made changes to her taste.

¼ cup flour
2 cups barbecue sauce
1 onion, sliced
2 tsp. chili powder
¼ tsp. cayenne
¼ tsp. garlic powder
1 tsp. dry mustard
1 large Reynolds Oven Bag™
3 lb. baby back ribs

Preheat the oven to 325 degrees.

Place the flour, barbecue sauce, onion, chili powder, cayenne, garlic powder, and mustard in the oven bag and mix.

Cut up the ribs and place them in the bag.

Tie the bag and shake to coat the ribs.

Make 6 slits in the bag.

Bake for $1^1/_2$ hours.

Serves 3 to 4.

Donna-Oh-Donna's Glazed Chicken

This recipe was named after Anthony and Gail's daughter Donna. When Donna was little, Gail would make this dish and call out, "Donna, oh, Donna!" Donna would come running to eat the glazed chicken.

1 tbsp. barbecue sauce
1 tbsp. mustard
1 1/2 tsp. red wine vinegar
1/2 tsp. hot sauce
Dash Worcestershire sauce
1 tbsp. olive oil
Salt
Black pepper
4 boneless, skinless chicken breasts

Combine the barbecue sauce, mustard, vinegar, hot sauce, and Worcestershire sauce in a bowl and mix well.

Lightly spray a skillet with nonstick cooking spray, and set on medium heat. Add the oil.

Sprinkle salt and pepper over the chicken.

Brush one side of the chicken with the sauce, and place sauce side up in the skillet. Flip the chicken over, and brush on more sauce.

Continue to flip over the chicken, and brush with the sauce.

Cook for approximately 15 minutes, or until the chicken is no longer pink inside.

Serves 4.

Notes

Anthony and Gail like to use Master Choice™ barbecue sauce.

Either Dijon or Creole mustard can be used.

Quick Breaded Chicken

This is a great recipe, because it is simple and requires little work yet results in a hot meal.

Oil
Egg Beaters™
Seasoned breadcrumbs
Salt (optional)
Black pepper (optional)
4 boneless, skinless chicken breasts

Pour oil in a skillet, and set on medium heat.

Pour Egg Beaters™ in a bowl.

Pour breadcrumbs in a separate bowl, and season if you desire with salt and pepper.

Dip the chicken in the Egg Beaters™, then in the breadcrumbs.

When the oil is hot, place the chicken in the skillet, and fry the breasts on each side until golden brown and cooked through.

Serves 4.

Chicken Casserole

The recipe is great for a dinner party.

2 cans cream of mushroom soup
2 cans cream of chicken soup
2 chickens (6 lb. each), cooked, deboned, and shredded
2 pkg. frozen broccoli spears, thawed
1 soup can water
2 small boxes raw minute rice
1 tbsp. minced onion
1 bottle (16 oz.) Cheez Whiz™

Mix all the ingredients together in a large bowl.

Preheat the oven to 350 degrees.

Spray a 9x13 baking dish with nonstick cooking spray. Place the mixture in the dish.

Bake for 45 minutes.

Serves 12.

Creole Chicken and Okra Over Rice

Notes

If you see that you do not have enough drippings from the chicken to make a roux, then add the other stick of butter.

More flour may be added to the roux if it is too soupy.

2 lb. frozen cut okra
6 pieces chicken (leg or breast)
Salt
Black pepper
1 to 2 sticks butter
$1/4$ to $1/2$ cup flour
1 bunch scallions, minced
1 onion, chopped
4 cloves garlic, chopped
1 can (8 oz.) tomato sauce
4 cups water
2 bay leaves
$1/4$ tsp. dried thyme
Cayenne
Cooked rice

In a skillet, cook the okra until it is no longer stringy.

Season the chicken with salt and pepper.

Melt 1 stick butter in a large pot. Place the chicken in the pot, and cook until the pieces turn brown on all sides.

Remove the chicken and place on a plate.

Reduce heat to medium low, and add $1/4$ cup flour. Constantly stir until it turns dark brown.

Add the scallions, onion, and garlic and sauté for 15 minutes.

Add the tomato sauce and cook for 5 minutes.

Slowly add the water, bay leaves, and thyme and bring to a boil.

Reduce the heat and let simmer. Place the chicken back into the pot and cook for 15 minutes.

Place the cooked okra in the pot, and cook for 30 minutes.

Add cayenne, salt, and pepper to taste.

Serve over rice.

Serves 8.

Supreme Casserole

2 cups chopped cooked chicken, beef, or shrimp
1 cup frozen peas, thawed
1 can (14¾ oz.) cream-style corn
¼ lb. American or cheddar cheese, cubed
1 small onion, chopped
1 cup evaporated milk
1 tbsp. Worcestershire sauce
½ tsp. salt
⅛ tsp. black pepper
Pinch cayenne
1 cup Bisquick™ mix
½ cup cornmeal
2 tbsp. sugar
1 egg

Combine in a mixing bowl the chicken or beef or shrimp, peas, corn, cheese, onion, ½ cup milk, Worcestershire sauce, salt, pepper, and cayenne.

Place the mixture in an 8-in. greased baking dish, and bake at 400 degrees for 10 minutes.

Combine the remaining ingredients and mix well.

Pour the mixture around the edge of the baking dish, leaving the center uncovered.

Bake for 20 minutes.

Serves 6.

Doohickey

When Anthony can't think of the name of something, he always calls it a "doohickey." Gail promised that one day she would name a recipe with this word. And here it is.

6 bamboo skewers
Medium to large shrimp with tails, peeled and deveined
Pineapple chunks
Grill Seasoning
2 tbsp. butter
2 tbsp. olive oil

Soak the skewers for 15 to 30 minutes in cold water.

Place 1 shrimp on a skewer, then 1 pineapple chunk, and continue this process to the end of the skewer.

Repeat this on the remaining skewers.

Sprinkle seasoning on each skewer.

Add the butter and oil to a skillet set on medium heat.

When the butter is melted, place the skewers in the skillet.

Cook on one side until the shrimp turn pink. Flip the skewers over, and cook until the shrimp turn pink on the other side.

Any juice left in the skillet can be poured over the skewers before serving.

Serves 6.

The recipe for Grill Seasoning can be found in Uglesich's Restaurant Cookbook.

The olive oil helps keep the butter from burning.

Doohickey Part II

This recipe includes a homemade sauce that adds more flavor to the original dish.

6 bamboo skewers
1 tbsp. lemon juice
1 tbsp. honey
1 tbsp. rum
Medium to large shrimp with tails, peeled and deveined
Pineapple chunks
Grill Seasoning
2 tbsp. butter
2 tbsp. olive oil

Soak the skewers for 15 to 30 minutes in cold water.

In a bowl, mix the lemon juice, honey, and rum.

Brush the mixture on each shrimp.

Place 1 shrimp on a skewer, then 1 pineapple chunk, and continue this process to the end of the skewer.

Repeat this on the remaining skewers.

Sprinkle the seasoning on each skewer.

Add the butter and oil to a skillet set on medium heat.

When the butter is melted, place the skewers in the skillet.

Cook on one side until the shrimp turn pink. Flip the skewers over, and cook until the shrimp turn pink on the other side.

Any juice left in the skillet can be poured over the skewers before serving.

Serves 6.

Notes

The recipe for Grill Seasoning can be found in Uglesich's Restaurant Cookbook.

The olive oil helps keep the butter from burning.

Tybee's Shrimp Burgers

This recipe is named after one of Gail's mom's best friends.

1 egg
1½ lb. small shrimp, peeled, deveined, and chopped
1 small onion, chopped
¼ cup chopped red bell pepper
2 stalks celery, chopped
1 tsp. salt
¼ tsp. black pepper
⅛ tsp. cayenne
1 tsp. baking powder
4 scallions, chopped
¼ tsp. chopped parsley
Vegetable oil
Flour

In the morning, beat the egg in a bowl, and add all the ingredients except the oil and flour. Mix well.

Cover and refrigerate.

In the evening, take the mixture from the refrigerator and make patties any size you like.

Cover the bottom of a skillet with oil and set on medium heat.

Dredge the patties in flour.

When the oil is hot, place the patties in the skillet and brown on both sides.

Drain on paper towels.

Serve on buns with any toppings of your choice.

Serves 8.

Shrimp-Stuffed Red Bell Peppers

1 cup raw rice (white or brown)
4 to 6 red bell peppers
1 lb. bulk Italian sausage (hot or mild)
1 medium onion, diced
1 lb. cooked shrimp, diced
1 can (10 oz.) Rotel™ diced tomatoes with green chilies
2 cups shredded Monterey Jack cheese

Cook the rice according to the package directions.

Cut the tops off the bell peppers, and remove the seeds.

Cut the bell peppers in half lengthwise, and drop the peppers in a pot of boiling water. Boil for 3 to 5 minutes.

Drain the bell peppers and let cool.

Place the sausage and onions in a large skillet and sauté until the sausage is cooked.

Add the cooked rice, shrimp, and tomatoes.

Add the cheese and cook until melted.

Stuff the bell peppers with the mixture and place them on a baking sheet.

Bake at 350 degrees for 15 minutes.

Serves 8.

Stuffed Cucumbers

$^1/_2$ lb. ground beef
$^1/_2$ lb. shrimp, peeled and deveined
1 stick butter
1 small onion, chopped
1 small green bell pepper, chopped
$^1/_4$ cup chopped celery
2 cloves garlic, chopped
1 cup seasoned breadcrumbs
1 egg, beaten
1 tsp. salt
$^1/_4$ tsp. black pepper
$^1/_8$ tsp. cayenne
6 cucumbers

Spray a skillet with nonstick cooking spray and brown the meat.

Drain the meat, and clean the skillet.

Spray the skillet again with nonstick spray, and sauté the shrimp until pink.

Remove the shrimp, and clean the skillet.

Add the butter to the skillet. Sauté the onion, bell pepper, celery, and garlic over medium heat.

Add the beef, shrimp, breadcrumbs (leave $^1/_4$ cup on the side), egg, salt, pepper, and cayenne. Mix well and cook for 5 minutes over low heat.

Cut the cucumbers in half lengthwise and scrape out the seeds.

Fill the cucumbers with the mixture.

Sprinkle the reserved breadcrumbs on top.

Note

Add more breadcrumbs if the mixture is too moist.

Place the cucumbers in a 9x13 baking dish, and pour some water in the dish to help prevent the cucumbers from sticking to the dish.

Bake the stuffed cucumbers at 300 degrees for 20 minutes.

Serves 12.

Cream of Shrimp Soup

1 to 2 tbsp. butter
4 scallions, chopped
2 cloves garlic, chopped
1 stalk celery, chopped
$\frac{1}{4}$ cup chopped green bell pepper
$\frac{1}{4}$ cup chopped red bell pepper
$\frac{1}{4}$ cup chopped yellow bell pepper
2 tbsp. medium sherry
1 qt. low-sodium chicken broth
$\frac{1}{3}$ cup raw rice
$\frac{1}{2}$ lb. medium shrimp, peeled, deveined, and chopped
1 bay leaf
1 tsp. dried thyme
2 tbsp. chopped parsley
$\frac{1}{2}$ to 1 cup heavy cream
$\frac{1}{2}$ to 1 tsp. salt
$\frac{1}{4}$ tsp. black pepper
$\frac{1}{8}$ tsp. cayenne

Melt the butter in a pot set on medium heat.

Add the scallions, garlic, celery, and bell peppers. Sauté for 5 minutes.

Add the sherry, and boil briefly.

Add the broth and rice. Continue to boil.

Reduce the heat, and simmer for 30 minutes,

Add the shrimp, and cook until they turn pink.

Turn off the stove, and when the mixture is cool, puree the mixture.

Pour the mixture back into the pot, and add the bay leaf, thyme, and parsley. Set on low heat.

Slowly add the cream and stir.

Add the salt, pepper, and cayenne.

Simmer for 5 to 10 minutes.

Serves 8.

Crab and Shrimp Stew

$^1/_2$ cup vegetable oil
$^3/_4$ to 1 cup flour
1 large onion, chopped
3 stalks celery, chopped
1 small green bell pepper, chopped
1 can (10 oz.) Rotel™ diced tomatoes with green chilies
10 cups water
1 tsp. Worcestershire sauce
1 tbsp. salt
$^3/_4$ tsp. black pepper
$^1/_4$ tsp. cayenne
2 lb. medium shrimp, peeled and deveined
1 lb. lump crabmeat
Cooked rice
2 scallions, chopped
3 tbsp. chopped parsley

Begin the roux by pouring the oil in a pot set on medium-low heat. Slowly add the flour, and constantly stir until dark brown.

Add the onions, celery, and bell pepper to the roux.

Sauté on low heat for 5 to 10 minutes.

Add the tomatoes and cook for 10 minutes.

Slowly add the water, Worcestershire sauce, salt, pepper, and cayenne. Cook for 20 to 30 minutes, still on low heat.

Add the shrimp and cook until they turn pink.

Add the crabmeat and cook for 3 minutes.

Adjust the seasonings as needed.

Serve over rice, sprinkled with scallions and parsley.

Serves 10 to 12.

Crab and Shrimp Stew

Crab Fritters

3 tbsp. butter
1 small onion, minced
1 clove garlic, minced
$1/4$ cup medium sherry
$1/2$ lb. claw crabmeat
1 tbsp. minced parsley
1 cup all-purpose flour
1 tsp. baking powder
1 tsp. salt
$1/2$ tsp. black pepper
$1/8$ tsp. cayenne
1 cup Egg Beaters™
Vegetable oil

In a skillet, melt the butter over medium heat.

Add the onion and garlic and sauté until limp.

Add the sherry, crabmeat, and parsley.

Cook over low heat for 5 minutes.

In a medium bowl, sift the flour and baking powder.

Add the salt, pepper, and cayenne.

Add the Egg Beaters™, and mix all by hand until smooth.

Add the garlic, onion, and crab mixture and blend by hand.

Cover with plastic wrap, and place in the refrigerator for 2 to 4 hours.

Pour oil in a skillet or fryer.

Heat the oil to 350 to 375 degrees.

Note

Egg Beaters™ is an egg substitute.

Take 1 tbsp. crab mixture and drop it into the oil. Add as many fritters as will fit (you may need to do this in batches). Fry until golden brown.

Place on a paper towel to drain.

Serves 2.

Crabmeat in Patty Shells

6 large frozen patty shells
$\frac{1}{2}$ stick butter
2 stalks celery, chopped
8 oz. fresh white mushrooms, sliced
2 scallions, chopped
2 tbsp. chopped red bell pepper
2 cans ($10\frac{3}{4}$ oz.) cream of mushroom soup
1 cup heavy cream or half-and-half
1 lb. jumbo lump crabmeat
2 tbsp. diced pimiento
1 tsp. salt
$\frac{1}{4}$ tsp. black pepper
$\frac{1}{8}$ tsp. cayenne

Bake the patty shells according to the package directions.

On low heat, melt the butter in a saucepan, and add the celery.

Add the mushrooms and cook for 5 minutes.

Add the scallions and bell pepper. Cook until tender.

Add the soup, cream, and crabmeat. Cook for 5 minutes.

Add the pimiento, salt, pepper, and cayenne and stir.

Fill the shells with the mixture.

Serves 6.

Creole Crab and Corn Bisque

This dish is great when the weather is cold. Anthony's birthday is in December, and Gail prepares this bisque for him every year.

Note

Use either yellow or white corn.

¾ cup butter
1 cup flour
3 tbsp. tomato paste
1 large onion, chopped
4 stalks celery, chopped
4 scallions, chopped
4 cloves garlic, chopped
1 green bell pepper, chopped
¼ cup chopped parsley
8 cups low-sodium chicken broth
1 tbsp. Worcestershire sauce
1 bay leaf
1 tbsp. chopped fresh thyme
2 tsp. salt
½ tsp. black pepper
¼ tsp. cayenne
1 tsp. ketchup
2 cups frozen corn, thawed
1 lb. lump crabmeat

In a stockpot set on medium heat, melt the butter.

Make a roux by adding the flour. Stir until golden brown.

Add the tomato paste and stir it into the roux.

Add the onion, celery, scallions, garlic, bell pepper, and parsley. Cook for 20 minutes.

Slowly stir in the chicken broth.

Add the Worcestershire sauce, bay leaf, thyme, salt, pepper, cayenne, and ketchup.

Add the corn and crabmeat. Cook for 15 to 20 minutes.

Taste if more seasoning is needed.

Serves 8 to 12.

Crawfish and Corn Chowder

Note

If you do not wish to make the chowder so rich, then substitute half-and-half or whole milk for the cream.

2 tbsp. butter or margarine
1 small onion, diced
¼ cup diced red bell pepper
1 stalk celery, diced
2 cloves garlic, chopped
1 lb. peeled crawfish tails
1 can (10 oz.) Rotel™ diced tomatoes with green chilies
1 cup fresh-shucked corn kernels
1 can (15¼ oz.) cream-style corn, white or yellow
2 tsp. salt
½ tsp. black pepper
¼ tsp. cayenne
1½ cups water
2 cups heavy cream
2 tbsp. chopped parsley

In a Dutch oven, melt the butter.

Add the onion, bell pepper, celery, and garlic, and sauté over low heat for 15 minutes, or until tender.

Add the crawfish and tomatoes. Blend, then cook for 5 minutes.

Add the corn kernels and creamed corn. Continue to cook on low heat for 10 minutes.

Add the salt, pepper, and cayenne.

Add the water and cream.

Blend, then simmer on low heat for 15 minutes.

Serve garnished with parsley.

Serves 8.

Veal Parmesan

1 stick butter, sliced into pats
Egg Beaters™
2 cups breadcrumbs
1 cup grated Parmesan cheese
6 veal cutlets
1 jar marinara sauce
6 thin slices mozzarella cheese

Set the oven at 325 degrees. Place the butter in a 9x13 baking dish and melt the butter in the oven.

Place Egg Beaters™ in a bowl.

Mix the breadcrumbs and Parmesan cheese together in a separate bowl.

Dip the veal in the Egg Beaters™ and then in the breadcrumbs.

Notes

Gail likes to use white veal in this recipe.

This veal is traditionally served alongside spaghetti.

Veal Parmesan

Place the veal in the dish and bake for 10 minutes.

Remove the dish and flip each cutlet over.

Bake for another 10 minutes.

Remove from the oven, and add a little marinara sauce on top of each cutlet. Then place 1 slice mozzarella on top of the marinara on each cutlet.

Return to the oven, and bake until the cheese melts.

Serves 6.

Gail's Lasagna

Gail makes this lasagna 3 times a year: for Donna and John's birthdays and for Christmas. The dish takes 3 days to prepare.

First Day
4 to 6 filet mignons (2 to 2½ in. thick)

Place the filet mignons in a skillet, set on medium heat, and cook until browned on both sides.

Remove the filets and drain on paper towels to remove all grease.

When cool, place in a bowl and refrigerate.

Second Day
Oil
1 medium onion, chopped
4 cloves garlic, chopped
1 can (12 oz.) tomato paste
1 can (28 oz.) crushed tomatoes
Salt
Black pepper
Water
½ to 1 cup imported Pecorino Romano cheese
½ to 1 cup sugar

Place the oil in a stockpot, and set on medium heat.

Add the onion and garlic, and sauté until soft.

Add the tomato paste, stir, and reduce heat to low. (Keep the can to measure the water.)

More water may be needed as the gravy cooks, if it becomes too thick.

When the gravy sits, it turns thick.

Cook down the paste for 1 hour. Stir frequently to make sure the paste does not burn.

Add the crushed tomatoes and cook down for 1 hour. (Keep the can again.) Stir frequently.

Add salt and pepper to taste.

Take the tomato paste can and fill it with water 3 times, pouring it into the stockpot.

Take the crushed tomatoes can, fill it with water once, and pour it into the stockpot.

Add the cheese, sugar, and more salt and pepper.

Stir and bring to a boil. Then reduce heat to medium low, put the cover on the pot, and cook for 1 hour.

Add the filets, cover the pot, and cook for another 2 hours.

While the gravy is cooking, taste it to see if more cheese, sugar, salt, or pepper are needed.

Remove the filets and shred them with your hands. Place in a bowl.

Place the gravy in a separate bowl, and refrigerate the filets and gravy.

Third Day
1 box lasagna noodles
15 oz. low-fat ricotta cheese
Shredded mozzarella cheese
Grated Parmesan cheese

Boil the lasagna noodles according to the package directions.

In a 9x13 baking dish, place a little of the gravy at the bottom, then layer on some noodles, meat, ricotta, and mozzarella.

Continue to make these layers until you have used all these ingredients.

Sprinkle Parmesan cheese on top.

Place the dish in a 350-degree oven.

Bake for 40 to 60 minutes.

Serves 10 to 12.

Gail's Lasagna

Macaroni Casserole

This is one of Gail's favorite dishes, and she often prepares it for guests at home.

1 lb. macaroni noodles
$1^{1}/_{2}$ lb. lean ground beef
1 medium onion, chopped
1 green bell pepper, chopped
1 can (12 oz.) tomato paste
1 can (28 oz.) crushed tomatoes
1 cup water
1 tsp. salt
$^{1}/_{2}$ tsp. black pepper
1 to 2 bay leaves
Softened butter
1 lb. Velveeta™ cheese, shredded
Pinch paprika
$^{1}/_{4}$ cup grated Parmesan cheese

Cook the macaroni according to the package directions.

While the macaroni is cooking, place the beef in a skillet set on medium heat. Add the onion and bell pepper and cook together.

Cook until the meat is no longer pink.

Add the tomato paste, crushed tomatoes, water, salt, pepper, and bay leaves. Simmer for 15 minutes.

Grease the bottom of a 4-qt. casserole with butter.

Place half of the cooked macaroni in the casserole.

Place half of the cooked meat on top of the macaroni.

Place half of the Velveeta™ cheese on top of the meat.

Gail like to use 93 percent lean ground beef in this dish, as well as penne or small shell pasta.

No oil is need in this recipe, as when the meat cooks, it releases enough fat to cook the vegetables.

Any leftovers can be frozen and reheated.

Place the rest of the macaroni on top, followed by the rest of the meat and Velveeta™.

Sprinkle the paprika and Parmesan cheese on top.

Set the oven at 350 degrees and bake the casserole for 45 minutes.

Serves 10.

Red Gravy for Pasta

Notes

If the sauce is too thick, add some water.

Cooked ground meat can also be added to create a meat sauce.

One of Anthony and Gail's favorite Italian restaurants is Tony Angelo's in New Orleans. Dining there inspired them to develop this recipe.

1 tbsp. olive oil
1 small white onion, diced
2 cloves garlic, minced
1/4 cup minced green bell pepper
1 can (28 oz.) whole peeled tomatoes
1 slice orange
1 slice lemon
4 leaves basil, chopped
1 tsp. salt
1/4 tsp. black pepper
1/4 tsp. sugar

Place the oil, onion, garlic, and bell pepper in a saucepan set on medium heat and sauté for 5 minutes.

Crush the whole tomatoes in a bowl and add to the saucepan.

Cook for 5 minutes.

Add the orange, lemon, basil, salt, pepper, and sugar.

Bring to a boil, reduce heat to low, and simmer for 30 minutes.

Serve over the pasta of your choice.

Serves 6.

Shrimp Ravioli

1 tbsp. olive oil
$\frac{1}{2}$ lb. small to medium shrimp, peeled, deveined, and tails removed
1 pkg. wonton wrappers
Egg Beaters™
Shredded mozzarella cheese
Marinara sauce

Add the oil to a skillet and set on medium heat.

Add the shrimp and cook until they turn pink.

Take 2 wrappers and brush the edges with Egg Beaters™.

Place 1 shrimp in the middle of 1 wrapper, and sprinkle with mozzarella cheese.

Place the other wrapper on top and squeeze the edges together to seal.

Continue the above process to fill all wrappers.

Fill a pot with water and boil.

Place the ravioli in the boiling water.

Cook for 10 to 15 minutes, or until the ravioli turn soft.

Place on plates and cover with marinara sauce.

Serves 3.

Notes

A beaten egg or olive oil can be used instead of Egg Beaters™.

If the shrimp are too large to fit into the wrappers, cut the shrimp in half or in pieces.

Chapter Three

Desserts

Following are some of our favorite homemade dessert recipes that our family prepares throughout the year.

Aunt Gloria's "Mrs. Fields Cookies™"

Aunt Gloria, Anthony's sister, would make these cookies, pack them in a tin can, and give them as Christmas presents.

1 lb. butter
4 cups old-fashioned Quaker™ oats
4 cups flour
2 cups granulated sugar
2 cups packed dark brown sugar
2 tsp. baking soda
2 tsp. baking powder
1 tsp. salt
2 tsp. vanilla
4 eggs
2 bags (12. oz each) chocolate chips
1 Hershey™ bar (8 oz.), melted

In a small pot, melt the butter.

Blend the oats in a blender until they are the consistency of flour.

Place the blended oats in a mixing bowl and add the flour, sugars, baking soda, baking powder, and salt.

Then add the melted butter, vanilla, eggs, chocolate chips, and melted chocolate bar. Mix well.

Using an ice-cream scoop, drop scoops of the dough onto 1 greased cookie sheet, 2 in. apart.

Heat the oven to 350 degrees, and bake the cookies for 11 to 13 minutes, or until slightly brown on the bottom. Let cool before removing from the cookie sheet.

Repeat the steps, until there is no more cookie dough.

Makes 6 dozen.

Note

If the cookies are too hard, place the desired amount in the microwave for 15 seconds to soften.

Chocolate Eclair Cake

This no-bake dessert is easy to prepare and perfect for the hot summer months. It came from Gail's sister, Marie.

1 large box instant vanilla pudding mix
1 container (8 oz.) Cool Whip™
1 cup sugar
1 box graham crackers
Chocolate frosting

Prepare the pudding according to package directions, and refrigerate.

When the pudding has chilled, in a mixer, combine the pudding, Cool Whip™, and sugar. Beat together until light and fluffy.

Line the bottom of an ungreased square baking pan with graham crackers.

Pour half of the mixture on top of the crackers.

Lay down another layer of crackers, and pour the rest of the mixture on top.

Place another layer of crackers on top.

Melt the chocolate frosting.

Pour and spread the frosting on top.

Refrigerate, covered with plastic wrap, for 1 day.

Serves 10.

Note

We use Duncan Hines™ chocolate frosting.

Nan's Angel-Food Pudding Cake

This recipe was developed by Gail's sister, Marie, who prepared this dessert for Donna and John on their birthdays. Marie's nickname is Nan. It is a great cake to make during summer, because it is light and cool.

1 box angel-food cake mix
1 large box instant chocolate pudding mix
1 container (8 oz.) chocolate whipped cream or topping

Prepare the angel-food cake according to package directions.

Prepare the pudding and refrigerate.

When the angel-food cake has cooled, take a bread knife and cut the cake in half crosswise.

Pour and spread the pudding on the cut side of the bottom half. Place the top half back on the cake and gently push it down on the pudding.

Completely cover the cake with the chocolate whipped cream.

Refrigerate for 1 day.

Serves 10.

Tiramisu

There are many variations of this famous dessert. This cake is John's wife's favorite and one he prepares for her birthday.

6 egg yolks
1¼ cups sugar
1¼ cups mascarpone cheese
1¾ cups heavy cream
3 pkg. (3 oz. each) ladyfingers
½ cup coffee liqueur
Cocoa powder

In the top of a double boiler, combine the egg yolks and sugar. Beat with a fork until thick.

Place water in the bottom of the double boiler and set it on medium-high heat.

When the water comes to boil, reduce the heat to a simmer.

Place the top of the double boiler over the simmering water, and stir the yolks for 10 minutes.

Remove the pan of yolks from the heat and let the mixture come to room temperature.

In a mixer, beat the mascarpone cheese. Add the cream and the yolk mixture.

Beat until fluffy.

Line the bottom and sides of a springform pan with ladyfingers.

Brush each ladyfinger with some coffee liqueur.

Pour half of the mixture on top of the ladyfingers.

Note

John uses Kahlua™ coffee liqueur.

Sprinkle with some cocoa powder.

Lay down another layer of ladyfingers.

Again brush each ladyfinger with some coffee liqueur.

Place and spread the remaining mixture on top of the ladyfingers.

Sprinkle with more cocoa powder.

Refrigerate for 1 day. Remove from the pan.

Serves 10.

Chocolate Lovers' Chocolate Cake

John wanted to develop a homemade chocolate cake. He research-
ed chocolate on the Internet and came up with this creation.

Cake
$2^3/_4$+ cups flour
1 cup cocoa powder
2 cups boiling water
1 cup unsalted butter
$2^1/_2$ cups sugar
4 eggs
1 tsp. vanilla
2 tsp. baking soda
$^1/_2$ tsp. baking powder
$^1/_2$ tsp. salt
$^3/_4$ cup milk-chocolate chips

Preheat the oven to 350 degrees.

Spray nonstick cooking spray on 3 cake pans. Sprinkle each with
some flour.

Mix the cocoa and water until smooth. Set aside to cool.

When it is cool, sift in $2^3/_4$ cups flour and set aside.

In a large mixing bowl, beat the butter, sugar, eggs, and vanilla
together.

Beat in the baking soda, baking powder, salt, and chocolate mixture.

Add chocolate chips and stir gently.

Pour the batter into the pans and bake for 30 minutes or until a
cake tester comes out clean.

Cool the cakes in the pans on wire racks for 2 hours, then turn out and complete cooling on the racks.

Filling

1½ cups heavy cream
½ cup confectioners' sugar
2 tsp. vanilla

Beat the ingredients together until stiff.

Frosting

1 cup unsalted butter
4 oz. unsweetened chocolate
2 oz. bittersweet chocolate
½ cup heavy cream
3¼ cups confectioners' sugar
½ cup chocolate shavings

Melt the butter and unsweetened and bittersweet chocolates together over low heat. Stir in the cream until smooth.

Using an electric hand mixer, beat in the sugar until the frosting holds stiff peaks.

Before you put the cake together, make sure that everything has completely cooled.

Spread the filling over 2 layers of cake.

Stack the 3 cakes together so that you have filling above the bottom and middle layers.

Frost the top and sides of the 3-layer cake. Decorate with chocolate shavings. Refrigerate for 1 day. When ready to serve, bring to room temperature.

After serving, refrigerate any leftover cake.

Serves 12.

Mama's Chocolate Fudge

Note

This fudge tastes even better 2 or 3 days after it is made.

Gail's mother, Jo, made one of three desserts every Christmas. She gave the fudge to family and friends as gifts. Upon completion of the dessert, she would always leave a little extra mixture for Donna and John to scrape from the pot.

3 cups sugar
2 tbsp. Hershey's™ cocoa
2 tbsp. dark Karo™ corn syrup
1 pkg. Jell-O™ chocolate fudge pudding mix
9 oz. Pet™ milk
½ stick butter
3 to 4 heaping tbsp. marshmallow creme
1 cup chopped pecans
12 pecan halves

Place the sugar, cocoa, syrup, Jell-O™, and milk in a pot. Set on medium heat and stir until everything has dissolved in the milk. Cook, stirring, until the mixture becomes bubbly. Continue to cook until the mixture reaches the soft-ball stage.

Test if the fudge is at the soft-ball stage by taking a small piece of the fudge and placing it in a cup of cold water. If the fudge forms a soft ball (but does not hold its shape), it is ready for the next step. If not, then continue to cook and retest until it is ready.

When the fudge is ready for the next step, add the butter and cook until the butter melts. Add the marshmallow creme and stir until everything is combined. Remove the pot from the stove.

Using a hand mixer, mix the ingredients and add the chopped pecans. Mix until everything is incorporated. Pour the fudge into a greased square pan. Place pecan halves on top of the fudge, approximately every 3 inches apart. When cool, cut into 12 pieces.

Serves 12.

Divinity

This white fudge was Jo's second Christmas dessert. She also gave this to family and friends as presents.

3 cups sugar
$^1/_2$ cup Karo™ light corn syrup
$^1/_2$ cup water
2 egg whites
1 tsp. vanilla
1 cup chopped pecans
12 pecan halves

Pour the sugar, syrup, and water in a pot.

Set on medium heat and stir until the sugar has dissolved. Cook, stirring, until the mixture becomes bubbly.

Continue to stir until the mixture becomes thick.

In the meantime, beat the egg whites with a hand mixer until foamy.

To test if the fudge is ready for the next step, place a small piece of the mixture in a cup of cold water. If the fudge forms a soft ball (but does not hold its shape), it is ready for the next step. If not, then continue to cook and retest until it is ready.

When the fudge is ready for the next step, fold the egg-white mixture into the fudge. Add the vanilla and chopped pecans and mix well.

Pour the fudge into a greased square pan.

Place pecan halves on top of the fudge, approximately every 3 inches apart.

When cool, cut into 12 pieces.

Serves 12.

Hamlets

This cookie recipe was Jo's third Christmas dessert. It was her husband Ed's favorite cookie. She named the cookies after a good friend, Mrs. Hamlet.

Notes

More flour may be needed to make the dough thick.

Ed used to dip the cookies in his coffee.

¾ cup light brown sugar
¾ cup granulated sugar
¾ cup Crisco™ shortening
2 eggs
1 tsp. cinnamon
1 tsp. ground cloves
1 tsp. nutmeg
1 tsp. baking soda
1 tsp. milk and 1 tsp. white vinegar, mixed well
1 cup chopped pecans
1 cup raisins
1 cup chopped dates
½ cup flour

Mix all the ingredients together except the flour.

Using a sifter, slowly add the flour to the mix.

Continue to stir until the dough becomes thick.

Take a spoonful of the dough and place onto a greased cookie sheet.

Continue, spacing the dough 1 in. apart, until the cookie sheet is full.

Bake at 350 degrees for 20 to 25 minutes until golden brown.

Makes 2 dozen.

Dynamo's Sweet-Potato Pie

Dynelle, Anthony and Gail's niece, makes this dessert every Thanksgiving. Her husband, Jack, gave her the nickname "Dynamo" because she is dynamic in the kitchen.

3 sweet potatoes
1/2 cup sugar
1 tsp. cinnamon
1 tsp. allspice
1/2 tsp. salt
3 eggs
1 cup milk
2 tsp. butter
1 graham-cracker pie crust

Cut the sweet potatoes in half and boil until soft. Peel the potatoes and mash until free of all lumps. Add the sugar, cinnamon, allspice, and salt. Mix well.

Beat the eggs in a separate bowl. Add the eggs to the mixture, and continue to mix.

Blend in the milk and butter. Continue to mix until creamy. Pour the mixture into the pie crust. Bake at 350 degrees for 40 to 45 minutes.

Whipped Cream

1 qt. heavy cream
1 tbsp. sugar

Mix the cream and sugar, and whip until fluffy. Let cool in the refrigerator.

Place a dollop on top of slices of the cooled sweet-potato pie.

Serves 12.

Any unused pie must be refrigerated.

Strawberry Sorbet

John saw a fruit sorbet recipe in *Parade* magazine. He played around with the ingredients and develped his own strawberry sorbet recipe.

Sugar Syrup
1 cup sugar
1 cup water

Pour the sugar and water into a saucepan, and set on medium heat.

Stir until the sugar dissolves.

Set aside and let cool.

Sorbet
2 lb. fresh strawberries
1 $^1/_4$ cups Sugar Syrup
2 tbsp. fresh orange juice
Mint leaves

Remove the strawberry stems and wash the strawberries.

Place the berries in a blender and add $^1/_4$ cup Sugar Syrup.

Blend until pureed.

Pour the mixture into a plastic freezer bowl. Add the remaining Sugar Syrup and the orange juice. Stir until mixed.

Freeze, then serve garnished with mint.

Serves 4.

Chapter Four

Uglesich's Last Full Day

Uglesich's was started by Sam Maté Uglesich in 1924 and soon became a New Orleans tradition. Sam's son, Anthony, worked at the restaurant for over 50 years, while Anthony's wife, Gail, contributed for more than 40.

Anthony and Gail's 24-hour, 7-days-a-week commitment to the restaurant helped propel Uglesich's to national prominence. One's weakness was the other's strength, so together they were perfect. In essence, Anthony and Gail are what made Uglesich's such a unique and successful restaurant.

However, the everyday grind of being hands-on restaurant owners was taking its toll on both of them. Uglesich's last full day of operation was May 5, 2005. Both felt that it was a sad yet joyous day, as they loved what they were doing, yet they were ready to cherish their memories.

Following are photographs of the restaurant's last full day, as seen through the eyes of Anthony and Gail's customers.

Uglesich's sign (Photo by Dynelle Rinkes)

Line outside of restaurant (Photo by Nancy Robinson Moss)

Diners outside the restaurant (Photo by Ray and Ellen Cook)

Uglesich's sign painted on the window (Photo by Chalon Viosca LaFleur)

Menu posted behind the counter (Photo by Chalon Viosca LaFleur)

Brown's Dairy, located across the street from Uglesich's, expresses their good wishes (Photo by Chalon Viosca LaFleur)

Fresh soft-shell crabs (Photo by Chalon Viosca LaFleur)

Fresh oysters (Photo by Chalon Viosca LaFleur)

Gail heads out to take orders (Photo by Chalon Viosca LaFleur)

Anthony autographs the first cookbook (Photo by Chalon Viosca LaFleur)

A table full of delicious Uglesich's food (Photo by Chalon Viosca LaFleur)

Fried soft-shell crab (Photo by Chalon Viosca LaFleur)

Fried oysters and shrimp (Photo by Chalon Viosca LaFleur)

Zena prepares food in the kitchen (Photo by Chalon Viosca LaFleur)

Skillets on the stove (Photo by Chalon Viosca LaFleur)

*Anthony and Gail are interviewed by a local television station
(Photo by Chalon Viosca LaFleur)*

Eddie Compass, police chief at the time, pays a final visit (Photo by Chalon Viosca LaFleur)

Customer Nancy Robinson Moss hugging Mike, the oyster shucker, goodbye. Over her shoulder, documentary director Karen Snyder and photographer Michael P. Smith can be seen. (Photo by Nancy Robinson Moss)

Carol Viosca, Chalon Viosca LaFleur, Leon Touzet, and Anthony share good-byes (Photo courtesy of Chalon Viosca LaFleur)

John Rea holds the last day's sales receipts (Photo by John Uglesich)

Anthony and Gail's last message (Photo by Chalon Viosca LaFleur)

Chapter Five

Uglesich's Survives Katrina

The City of New Orleans issued a mandatory evacuation order when Hurricane Katrina threatened to make landfall on the Louisiana/Mississippi Gulf Coast. The city and its citizens would forever be affected, with many, including some of our own family members, losing their homes and possessions.

Anthony's mother, Emily, celebrated her 100th birthday in Memphis, Tennessee. She passed away on March 21, 2007, never able to return to her home in New Orleans, which was destroyed.

Although Uglesich's had closed almost four months before the hurricane, Anthony had continued to keep up the restaurant property. Like Anthony and Gail's house, it sustained damage to its roof in the storm and lost all of its food, refrigerators, and freezers afterwards. Both the restaurant and their home were spared from any flooding.

Images of the massive flooding, people stranded on their rooftops, destroyed homes, and the Superdome have been beamed around the world. We want to focus on the outreach of love and support from customers offering us their thoughts, prayers, and even use of their own homes.

Following are some of the e-mails we received in the aftermath of Katrina, which struck on August 29, 2005. We responded to each and every e-mail.

May God bless you all.

Re: Hurricane

August 30, 2005

Hi, Mr. and Mrs. U and John. Stacey and Christine here in San Diego checking on you all. Hoping you are all okay. If you need anything please let us know. You are always welcome here in San Diego if you need to. Please let us know if we can do anything.

Our thoughts and prayers are with you.

Stacey and Christine

Re: News

August 31, 2005

All of your friends in Chicago hope that everyone is safe.

John N.

Re: Need Anything?

August 31, 2005

I don't know if you guys are getting any communication or not. Just wanted to see if there was a way to send you any water, wipes, disinfectant, etc., that you may need. Hope y'all are safe. Hope to be back; take care.

Rusty R., North Carolina

Re: Hi from Mike

August 31, 2005

Hi Gail and Anthony,

If there's anything I can do . . . if anyone from Uglesich's needs [something] now and during reconstruction, please let me know. I tried to call but there was no answer. Standing by to help.

Mike H.

Re: Hello from the Johnsons in Oakland

August 31, 2005

Dear Anthony, Gail, John, and Donna,

We hope that you are all safe and well. If we can do anything to help, please let us know.

Maybe now is a good time for a visit to California. We have a home in South Tahoe that is available.

You're all welcome anytime.

Take care,
Terry and LuNell

Re: Call Us

August 31, 2005

Greetings Anthony and Gail,

Extending our thoughts and prayers to you and yours. If you or anyone in your company is in need of a home, please feel free to contact me. My wife and I have ample space to accommodate at least 4. At your convenience, please drop us a line to let us know your situation.

Prayerfully yours,
Ken and Sharon C.
Missouri

Re: Anthony and Gail

September 1, 2005

Here in Atlanta, we're all praying for you. We hope you are safe, and know how many people everywhere care for you.

God bless you,
Jack W. and Janet W.
Paul and Dorothy S.
Lynn and Candace F.
Raad and Karena C. in Pensacola
Bill and Sandy W. in Minneapolis

Re: Are You OK

September 1, 2005

I've been trying to get in touch with as many of my New Orleans friends as possible in the past couple of days. It's impossible to call anybody in the 504 area code. I hope you and your folks are somewhere safe. I'm guessing that the old restaurant probably got washed away. Please let me know whenever this reaches you.

We're donating some money to the Red Cross but the scope of this tragedy is overwhelming.

All the best. God bless.

Cary W.

Re: This Should Make You Feel a Little Better

September 1, 2005

Dear John,

I just want you, your sister, and your parents (and your dear puppy) to know we think of you every minute of every day. Your beautiful city is in shambles and although the most important thing is that you are safe, it is still so sad to see such a wonderful place brought to this. I consider New Orleans the heart and soul

John, Anthony, and Gail with Borders district marketing manager Vicki Lorini and her husband, Tom, at a book-signing event in Sacramento before Katrina.

of our country. It's the conduit for our friendship and so many wonderful memories. It will be reborn and we will do what we can to help. It just makes me want to cry.

In the meantime, please consider our home in California as a refuge if you want. It's not too big, but we would always welcome you. I hope you are all staying well and somehow managing in this unbelievably challenging time. It's people like you who will make New Orleans live on.

Love,
Vicki L.
Borders Group Inc.

Re: Is Everyone All Right?

September 1, 2005

Hello:

A note here from a faithful fan. We've been following the events down by y'all and you've been in our thoughts.

We pray everyone is all right.

Best,
Danny B., NYC

Re: Our Prayers Are with All of You

September 1, 2005

We have been to your restaurant many times and own your cookbook and just feel so helpless except to send money. Don't even know if the restaurant is there anymore, but if there is anything we can do in Newman, Georgia, let us know. We have a shelter here and we can take people into personal homes here as well.

We are praying earnestly and specifically for each and every one of you.

Pat and Janet F.

Re: Thinking about You

September 1, 2005

Hi friends,

You don't know me, but I saw you once on Emeril Live and I liked you all. You and your well being have been on my mind and I just want you to know my prayers are with you and all who have been affected by this horrible storm. I hope you are all OK.

Your friend,
Darcy K.

Re: From Kiss My Ribs BBQ

September 2, 2005

Don't know when anyone will be able to check e-mail, but our thoughts and prayers are with all of you.

God bless,
Mike (barbeque man) and Vicky W.

Re: OK?

September 2, 2005

Anthony and Gail,
I don't know if you'll get this or if you have time to answer, but we have been concerned about all our New Orleans friends. We hope you are ok. Erin was at Tulane this summer until about two weeks before the storm, then she left to start her job in San Francisco. We were so lucky.

If you have time to reply, let us know how you are. If you are in Houston, we have plenty of room for you to stay at our house.

Your friends,
Bill, Rosanna, Erin, Sarah, and Caity

Re: Is Everyone OK?

September 3, 2005

Hi there,

I'm sure you've been inundated with e-mails about the staff but I'm wondering if Gail and Tony are safe and sound as well as Michael & Anthony . . . any word from any of them?

Please let them know their San Francisco fans are keeping them in our thoughts and prayers . . . and if there is anything we can offer to let us know!

Susan B. & Jazz Fest friends

Re: Are You OK?

September 4, 2005

Just a person who comes to your restaurant whenever I can. I hope you are ok.

Courtney

Re: Calling from Detroit

September 5, 2005

We are hoping and praying that you are all right. We have not stopped thinking about our friends in N.O., but we haven't been able to reach anyone. If you get a chance, drop us an e-mail or even a note on your website.

We own a three bedroom cottage on Cape Cod that is equipped to be used year round. It will be available after the beginning of October if any of you need it. Give our best to Anthony, Gail and, as Anthony calls her, Momma.

Donna and P.J.

Re: Our Prayers Are with You

September 5, 2005

Dear Anthony and Gail,

We only pray that this e-mail finds you and your loved ones safe. If there is any way that we can help directly PLEASE let us know. Indeed we do know what it means to miss New Orleans. We have a 3 bedroom vacation rental house and a 1 bedroom vacation cottage here in our property in Hayesville, NC. We always told you that you were welcome anytime, as our guests. We extend that offer again, for as long as needed. Know that you all are in our thoughts and prayers. You have given us such joy, in amazing culinary delights throughout the years, along with your warm welcome. We feel like y'all are family.

If you get this, please let us know that you're okay.

With love,
David and Kirsten G.

Re: Are You OK?

September 6, 2005

One of our fondest memories of our 2001 trip to New Orleans was lunch at Uglesich's. We had read about you and seen you on Martha Stewart's TV show. We ate at all the "famous" New Orleans restaurants and by far had the best food of our trip with that lunch with you.

With all of the reports of the devastation in New Orleans we have thought of you and your tiny restaurant often. It is our hope that you and your family are all personally safe and that your loss has not been as devastating as some. We would love to hear from you and hope that you plan to reopen at some point.

Bless you . . .
George and Linda D.
San Jose, California

Re: Can We Help?

September 6, 2005

We have been trying to contact you via phone to see if you and your family are safe.

Laurie S. has tried to call you. Laurie talked to Paul V. and he and his friends are safe staying with friends and relatives. I thought I would try this e-mail address. You are all in our thoughts and prayers. We hope you are all safe. Please let us know if we can help with anything.

Love,
Janet C.

Re: Our Prayers Are with You

September 6, 2005

Dear Anthony, Gail, and All,

You are constantly and will remain in our prayers. Just say the word and the houses are ready for you. It's a beautiful September here in the mountains, and the property is situated on the shores of a 7000 acre lake, surrounded by the Smoky Mountains. A great place to restore one's spirit. Should you decide to take us up on our offer and are driving, we will give directions; if flying, we would be happy to pick you up at any of those airports.

Love,
Kirsten and David G.

Re: How Are You?

September 7, 2005

I am one of a group of loyal fans from California, and am wondering how you have survived the storm and its aftermath. Please let us know how you are.

Just know that there is a large group of people out in California praying especially for you and your family. Please let us know if there is another way we can help.

Judy T.

Re: Our Thoughts Are on N.O.

September 8, 2005

My friends and I frequent your restaurant each time we are in town. I was wondering how the restaurant, your family and employees fared in the flood. Hope all is well and we look forward to seeing you again next year.

Best regards,
Steve S.

Re: Notes from Glenside PA

September 8, 2005

Dear Miss Gail and John,

We met this spring at the Gerhard's demonstration when you came to Philly for the Book and the Cook. I know your restaurant is closed this time of year. I wanted to drop you a note and let you know I was thinking of you and hoping you and your business are safe.

All the best to you and your patrons as they try to rebuild.

Warm regards,
Amy W.

Re: Status

September 8, 2005

Are you ok?

A friend and patron

Re: Hope You Are OK!

September 10, 2005

I hope you're well and in good company. I enjoyed your restaurant in the past and look forward to another visit. Sorry your great city has had so much misfortune but you have lots of support from all of us Americans.

Take Care
R. P.

Re: We're So Glad to Hear You're All OK

September 11, 2005

Gail & Anthony & John:
I got Janet's e-mail from John that you're all OK. We just wanted to let you know how much we're thinking of you and that we're so glad to hear that you're all safe. I've tried to call on your cell phone, but have never been able to get through. We know that you probably don't know much about what's going on with everything, but if there is anything we can do to help you, either now or in the future, please let us know. We wish you all the best and we're so happy you're all fine.

Laurie & Vance S.

Re: Condition of Restaurant, Family & Staff

September 12, 2005

Dear Uglesich's

Just wanted to know how your restaurant has fared during Katrina. Our daughter is a graduate of Tulane and we have been big fans for several years. We always visit for crab cakes and a Bloody Mary when we are in town and have introduced many of our friends here in Texas to your wonderful food and hospitality.

We hope all of your family and staff are fine. Please know that you are in many people's thoughts and prayers.

Cathey M.
Austin, Texas

Re: With Concern

September 12, 2005

Gail and Tony:

In the wake of Katrina, we are worried about you—we came to treasure the Uglesich family in our recent visits to New Orleans. Of course, right now, none of you are present at Uglesich's, but we want to reach out in an attempt to let you know that we are thinking of each and every one of you that touched our lives this year (March 2005) and last year (March 2004). We sincerely care for your troubles in this devastating time. Anthony, we hope that you had a successful knee replacement surgery and that Gail, you have had successful surgery on your wrist; we're afraid we contributed to the strain on your wrist in making those Bloody Marys! We think of you often and pray that you are safe and well, despite the undoubted tragedy that you are living through.

For you and your enthusiastic and talented staff, we send positive energy and caring prayers. You have touched our lives and we hope that our thoughts of you will touch you as well.

Be well and stay safe. Please let us know how we can best support the recovery of New Orleans.

Ted & Laura R.
Cortland, New York

Re: Arkansas Concern for You All

September 13, 2005

Gosh, [have] been praying diligently for the entire Uglesich family!! Doubtful you remember us, but we ate 4 consecutive lunches with you all in January. . . . Your cookbooks were a hit with all three of our sons and their wives and we are trying the courage to have a Uglesich Cookoff! We just need Y'ALL's special touch!

Take care and PLEASE let us know if we can be of assistance in any way! DO NOT hesitate to call us if we can be of help to ANYone!

Concerned and so grateful to you all for incredible memories (and looking forward to many more!).

Please know we support you with our thoughts and prayers and would be truly honored to assist you at this difficult time. We have several families of wonderfully appreciative evacuees here in our little Arkansas town. Our heart aches for them and all coastal residents. They are amazing! Mississippi is my home and so many precious memories are because of our gulf coast and NOLA!

We do know how to share and happily so. While waiting to return to NOLA you are more than welcome to join us and experience our cotton harvest! We will even COOK for you all! Not promising Shrimp Uggie but we set a "fairly filling keep the farmer happy" dinner table!

Patsy and Witt S.
Blytheville, AR

Re: Sending Love

September 13, 2005

I am so hopeful all is well with you? You are such an important place in the country. I have not heard anything about how you survived. Bless you all.

Sherry S.

Re: From Faye

September 16, 2005

Hoping all of your family and properties are okay and were not hurt from Hurricane Katrina.

I heard you closed at the end of the summer. Is this true? Is it for good or just until spring or so? Do you have any t-shirts and cookbooks left?

Thank you.
Faye H.

Re: I Hope You and Your Family Are OK?

September 19, 2005

Thanks for the wonderful cookbook. I've made 40% of the dishes.

I just returned from 2 weeks in Biloxi helping my sister and friends.

The destruction was awful in so many ways, but the spirit of the people is great. I hope you and your family can return to New Orleans and help its re-birth. New Orleans without [Uglesich's] isn't New Orleans.

Donald E.
New Mexico

Re: How Are You? We Hope Well

September 20, 2005

One of the highlights of our 2005 honeymoon in New Orleans was the lunch we had at your restaurant. My wife and I were the first to arrive that morning and Tony welcomed us and let us in. He made us feel like we were customers and friends for 30 years as he sat with us, asked us what we basically liked/disliked and then decided what he would make us for lunch. Needless to say, we were not disappointed! It was one of the most wonderful meals we have ever had! We treasure the autographed cookbook as well.

Try as we might, we have not been able to find any information out on the web to see if you and your staff weathered the storm all right (we've prayed for you all often) and hope that you and yours are safe and sound.

God bless you all.
Jerry & Deb O.
Williamsville, NY

Re: Flooding

September 25, 2005

I have been staring at maps and satellite photos, trying to figure out whether the neighborhood around your restaurant flooded or not after Hurricane Katrina. From the satellite photos, it looks like the waters didn't go further south than Rampart/Simon Bolivar. Did your restaurant survive? Will it reopen?

Sincerely,
Cehwiedel

Re: Great Cookbook

May 8, 2006

I lost my cookbook in Lakeview due to flooding. When I was deciding which books needed to be replaced first, I put *Uglesich's Cookbook* in the top five even though I had only owned it a few months before the flood. The *Uglesich's Cookbook* is one of the finest New Orleans cookbooks for the home cook. The instructions are straightforward and there are no fussy ingredients. The results define the best in New Orleans cuisine.

Libby B.
Lakeview—New Orleans

Re: Washington

March 1, 2006

Just wanted to check and see if you guys are okay and still standing? This was the best food in New Orleans. We will be back!

Seoma
Mukilteo
Washington

Index